Jess AND Layla's Astronomical Assignment

Written by Lucy Courtenay

Illustrated by Ben Whitehouse

Acknowledgments
The publisher would like to thank the following for their kind permission to reproduce their photographs: (Key: b-bottom; c-center; l-left; r-right; t-top) Alamy Images: PRISMA ARCHIVO 61r; Getty Images: DeAgostini 61l

All other images © Pearson Education

Every effort has been made to trace the copyright holders and we apologize in advance for any unintentional omissions. We would be pleased to insert the appropriate acknowledgment in any subsequent edition of this publication.

PEARSON

ISBN-13: 978-0-328-85390-8
ISBN-10: 0-328-85390-9

5   16

Contents

Achoo!

The smell of the science laboratory was tickling Layla's nose. It was no good, she was going to . . .

"ACHOO!"

"Bless you," said Dr. Goggles at the front of the class.

"Thank you, Dr. Goggles," said Layla, and then quickly, "sorry, Dr. Goggles."

How embarrassing, she thought as everyone started laughing.

"Jess," she whispered to her best friend, "I think I'm allergic to Science."

Jess peered at Layla through her bangs and sighed. "Layla, you can't be allergic to a subject."

"I can," Layla said. "I never sneeze in History, do I?"

Jess looked thoughtful as she twirled her bangs between her fingers. "I do get hiccups a lot in History," she said.

"See?" said Layla. "Allergic."

"Today, we are learning about astronomy," Dr. Goggles told the class.

Layla nearly jumped out of her seat with excitement. "I love astronomy, Dr. Goggles!" she said. "My mother is a Scorpio."

Before long, the whole class was talking about zodiac signs. Danny Philips was a Taurus, Jade Jefferson was a Capricorn, and Jess was a Leo, just like Layla. Their birthdays were two days apart, and their mothers had met in the hospital; they had been best friends ever since.

"Zodiac signs are *astrology*, Layla," said Jess, "not *astronomy*. Astronomy means 'the law of the stars;' it's a different subject."

"Oh," said Layla in disappointment as she rubbed her nose, which was tickling again.

"That's right, Jess," said Dr. Goggles, "and to understand astronomy, we must first look at history."

Layla's nose stopped tickling at once and she sat up. She loved history. She leaned forward so she could hear every word that Dr. Goggles was saying.

"People have wondered about the Sun, the Moon, Earth, and the stars since the beginning of time," Dr. Goggles began. "In ancient Egypt, people believed the Sun was a god called Ra, and there are Sun and Moon temples in cultures all over the world."

"My mom worships the Sun," said Layla. "We always go to the beach in the summer." Jess let out a giggle, and Dr. Goggles shot the pair of them a stern look.

"We understand more about astronomy these days," continued Dr. Goggles, "but people in the past had unusual ideas."

Dr. Goggles then showed the class a picture of a marble sculpture of a bearded man.

"This is Thales, who lived in ancient Greece more than 2,500 years ago. Thales thought Earth was flat, like a plate."

Layla thought about the horizon. It did look pretty flat, so she could see why Thales had made this mistake. Then she pictured the sea running off the sides of the Earth like overflowing soup—wait, that would never work!

"There were, however, other scientists living at the same time as Thales who thought differently about Earth," said Dr. Goggles, showing the class another picture.

"Anaximander, for example, thought that Earth was cylindrical—in other words, shaped like a can of beans."

Layla raised her hand and asked, "Did Thales and Anaximander know each other, Dr. Goggles?"

"Thales was Anaximander's teacher," Dr. Goggles replied.

"I bet they argued a lot," Jess whispered to Layla.

"I bet Thales put Anaximander in detention for answering back," Layla whispered back.

Dr. Goggles was still talking. "Anaximander influenced another important Greek astronomer called Pythagoras," she continued, "and Pythagoras believed that crystal spheres spun around Earth. The crystal spheres held the Sun, the Moon, the stars, and the planets, and he believed that when the spheres touched each other, you could hear music."

Musical crystal spheres sounded pretty, thought Layla, imagining wind chimes hanging in space, chiming against each other.

"These two men are Aristotle and Aristarchus," said Dr. Goggles, tapping two more pictures on her interactive screen. "They lived more than one hundred years after Pythagoras. Aristotle, was a very clever scientist who proved that Earth was a sphere, not the shape of a can of beans. However, he still believed the Sun moved around Earth, while Aristarchus thought Earth moved around the Sun. Who do you think was right?"

"Aristarchus, obviously!" said Jess, rolling her eyes.

"Well, that sounds obvious now," said Dr. Goggles, "but it wasn't so obvious two thousand years ago before we had the scientific knowledge we have today. The world believed Aristotle for 1,600 years until Nicolaus Copernicus came along."

"My brother has a friend named Nicolaus," called out Danny Philips, to no one in particular.

"My dog's name is Copernicus," Jade Jefferson joined in, "but we call him 'Copper' for short."

"My dog's name is Waffles, and we call him 'bad dog' for short," giggled Layla.

Dr. Goggles cleared her throat, and the class quickly stopped talking about their pets.

"Nicolaus Copernicus was born in 1473 in Poland," she said. "Like Aristarchus, he believed that Earth revolved around the Sun; this theory is known as heliocentrism. A hundred years after Copernicus, an astronomer named Galileo tried to prove that Copernicus's ideas were correct, but Galileo was arrested in 1633 for suggesting that Earth wasn't at the center of the universe."

Layla sat up. "Did he go to jail, Dr. Goggles?" she asked.

"Not exactly," Dr. Goggles said, "but after refusing to give up his beliefs he was eventually placed under house arrest. The authorities wanted to keep a close eye on him!"

"I'd like to be under house arrest," said Danny Philips, "Then I could watch TV all day long."

"They hadn't invented TV in 1633, Danny," said Jess, rolling her eyes at Layla.

Just then, the bell rang. "Right, before you go—
homework time!" said Dr. Goggles, and everyone in
the class groaned. Ignoring the groans, she began.
"I want you to imagine what would happen if all the
astronomers we have talked about today got together
for a dinner party. What would they argue about?
Would they make friends with each other? And would
they learn anything new? What do you think they
would say if you told them what we know now about
their theories? I'd like you to write one page about
this, and you can work in pairs if you'd like. Now off
you go, and I'll see you next week!"

Looking at the Past

Layla had a big bedroom at the top of her house, with one window overlooking the road and a skylight in the ceiling. Waffles, her small, scruffy dog, was lying on her bed and snoring.

"Get off my bed, Waffles," said Layla, and then she added, "bad dog!"

Waffles opened one eye and peered up at Layla, but showed no interest in moving, so instead the two friends lay side by side on Layla's green bedroom rug and gazed up toward the sky through the skylight.

"Let's look for homework inspiration among the stars," Jess suggested.

"But there aren't any stars," said Layla.

"That's because it's still too light to see them," said Jess, "but if we keep looking, they'll start coming out in a minute."

The longer the girls lay on the rug, the darker the sky became, as one little star blinked into view, followed by another, and then two more. Soon the whole sky was freckled with tiny pinpoint lights. Waffles snored loudly from the bed beside them.

"Did you know we're really looking at the past when we look up at the stars?" Jess said, dreamily.

"But we're looking at the stars now," Layla said, confused, "and now isn't the past."

"Stars are millions of light years away from Earth, though," explained Jess. "Some of the stars we're looking at don't even exist anymore because they exploded a million years ago, and we're only just seeing the light. So, we're looking at the past."

"How fast does light travel?" Layla asked.

"About 186,000 miles per second," said Jess.

"And how many seconds are there in a year?"

"31,536,000," Jess answered. She loved science facts.

"So if light travels at 186,000 miles per second, and there are 31,536,000 seconds in a year . . ." Layla could feel her brain frying as she tried to imagine how far light traveled in one year; she didn't dare try to imagine millions of light years!

"Wow," she said, feeling a little weak.

"It's cool, right?" said Jess.

"I wish we really could go back in time," said Layla. "I would find all those old astronomers and show them everything we know about the solar system today— what a surprise they would get!"

Jess suddenly lifted her arm and pointed as a bright light flashed across the sky. "You just wished on a meteor, Layla!" she said.

Layla sat up, blinking. "Wasn't that a shooting star?"

"It's the same thing, silly," Jess replied. "A meteor or shooting star is the bright flash you see when a meteoroid burns through the atmosphere."

"What's the difference between a meteor and a meteoroid?" asked Layla.

"A *meteoroid* is a piece of rock that has broken off a comet or an asteroid as it flies through space," Jess said, "and a *meteor* is the burning light that you see when a meteoroid reaches Earth's atmosphere. And when a meteoroid hits Earth, then it's a *meteorite.*"

19

"Meteoroid, meteor, meteorite," Layla repeated. Then she said dreamily, "Do you think it might come true, Jess, my wish about traveling back in time?"

"I doubt it, Layla—time travel is scientifically impossible," said Jess in a matter-of-fact way.

"But Thales thought it was impossible for Earth to be round," Layla pointed out, "and Aristotle thought it was impossible for the Earth to travel around the Sun."

"That's different," said Jess, although she sounded a little uncertain.

"Could it be," said Layla, "that it's just that we haven't discovered time travel yet?"

The sky was suddenly filled with shining golden rain as twenty or more meteors fizzed, sparkled, and flew through the air, followed by a series of three flashes.

BANG! There was a sudden clunk and a thud that came from the front of the house. Waffles yelped and sprinted out of the room with his tail between his legs as Layla and Jess scrambled to their feet, ran to the bedroom window, and looked out into the front yard.

"No way!" Layla said in disbelief, turning to look at Jess. "I think a meteorite just hit my dad's old van!"

Layla's dad had an old red van that was covered in rust, with brown seats full of moth holes, but Layla loved the van because her family went camping in it and drove it out for picnics in the summer. As she looked at it now, it seemed to be glowing like an ember and smoking gently.

Layla rushed down the stairs two steps at a time with Jess following close behind her. They skidded out the front door into the front yard, where lights were sparkling up and down the van's rusty red hood. As the girls hesitated, not sure what to do next, the van's passenger door swung open with a creak.

Layla's stomach started fizzing.

"Jess," she said, "I think the van wants us to get in."

Jess looked at Layla oddly. "Vans don't *want* things, Layla, they're *vans*."

Layla's stomach was fizzing more strongly. "I don't think it's a van anymore," she said. "I think something weird is going on."

Layla climbed inside and Jess followed closely behind her. Everything looked the same—holey brown seats, big gear shift, rusty pedals—but *something* was different.

"What's wrong with that clock?" asked Jess as she climbed into the van beside Layla. The digital clock display read U R IN 2015.

"Oh, that old thing has never worked," said Layla, staring through the window. "When it's 8:15 it says it's 3:29, when it's 8:42 it says it's 9:36—it just does whatever it wants!"

Jess looked at Layla. "But it's not even saying a time, Layla—it says U R IN 2015, look!"

Layla looked at the clock, paused, and then let out a gasp. "Oh, wow, Jess," she said, "what if my wish on the meteor came true? What if my Dad's van just turned into a time machine?"

"Or maybe the clock is just super broken," said Jess, folding her arms.

Layla sighed. Jess was very smart—she liked facts, not imagination. It was a good thing that Layla had more than enough imagination for them both.

Telescopes and Squabbles

"A time machine is impossible," Jess said again, pausing between each word.

"But I wished on a meteor," protested Layla.

"Yes, but—"

"I wonder what will happen if I fiddle with the knobs on the clock," Layla interrupted Jess. "Maybe I can turn it back to 1633."

"And why would you want to do that, exactly?" Jess asked flatly. This was getting ridiculous—didn't Layla know they had homework to do?

"Because 1633 was the year Galileo was arrested," said Layla triumphantly.

"Nothing will happen if you change that clock, Layla," Jess said impatiently.

"Then you won't mind if I do it, will you?"

Layla reached for the little knobs that changed the time on the clock.

"Don't touch it!" said Jess, suddenly nervous, as she twisted her bangs between her fingers.

"Don't be scared, Jess," Layla reassured her friend. "Wouldn't it be fantastic if we found Galileo? I feel bad that he was put under house arrest when he was right all along. We could prove his theory was correct and change the course of history!" Then as an afterthought she added, "And it would help with our homework project."

Jess covered her face with her hands. "I suppose scientists do experiments," she said through her fingers, "and this is an experiment, right?"

Layla nodded . . . and twisted the clock all the way back to 1633.

The van started to shake as the engine roared to life. Lights flickered along the dashboard, the headlights came on, and the van lifted off the ground and started to twist up into the air. Suddenly Layla couldn't tell if they were going backward or forward, up or down.

"This is like being on a roller coaster!" shrieked Layla.

"I don't like roller coasters, and I don't like this either!" Jess shouted back.

Around and around they spun, as if they were in a giant red washing machine, until finally there was a loud **BANG!** as the van hit the ground and the headlights lost power.

Layla peered hazily through the windshield.

"It's too dark to see where we are," she said, disappointed, "or *when* we are."

"You could try to switch the headlights back on," Jess suggested in a shaky voice.

Layla switched on the headlights, and as they flickered to life, they saw that the van had appeared in a room with straw matting on the floor and a large wooden telescope on a table by the window.

An old man sat up in bed and blinked in the bright lights.

"Are you angels?" he asked as Jess and Layla climbed out of the van.

"Hardly," said Jess, amused by the fact they might be described as angelic.

"I'm Layla," said Layla, pushing past Jess, "and this is my friend Jess. Are you Galileo?"

The old man jumped out of bed, adjusting his nightcap and smoothing out his nightshirt. "Yes, I am, but no one is allowed in my chamber," he said in a fussy voice. "I am under arrest and if anyone catches you in here, I will be in trouble."

31

"Let's face it, Galileo," said Layla, "you're in quite a lot of trouble already."

"And anyway, your arrest is nonsense, because the theory about heliocentrism is right," said Jess, interrupting.

Galileo looked amazed. "How do you know about heliocentrism? Girls don't study astronomy," he said.

"These girls do," said Layla, "and if you come with us, you can meet Nicolaus Copernicus. I know you two will like each other. When did Dr. Goggles say Copernicus was born, Jess?"

"Copernicus was born in 1473," Jess recited, "so let's go back to around 1510."

"What on earth are you talking about—Nicolaus Copernicus has been dead for almost a hundred years!" Galileo spluttered. "Meeting him is simply impossible!"

"He's as bad as you—no imagination," Layla said to Jess, and then to Galileo, "I promise you'll have a great trip, Galileo."

Galileo looked at the old red van. "Your horse has very bright eyes," he said doubtfully, "are you sure he's safe?"

Jess and Layla tried to stifle their laughter as they helped Galileo into the van.

"My telescope!" Galileo cried as he ran to fetch the long brown telescope from the table and carry it carefully back to the van.

"I can't leave my telescope behind," he said as Layla fixed his seat belt. "It is very valuable. A Dutchman invented the telescope, but I improved it with this one so that I could study the stars. I bet you have never seen one before." Galileo looked so proud that Layla didn't have the heart to tell him that she had a telescope at home.

"1510, here we come!" she said instead, and she twisted the dial on the clock.

This time, the van landed in a cobbled backyard in daylight, where an old man in a long red cloak with a black fur collar stared at them in astonishment.

Galileo threw open the van door. "Copernicus!" he gasped as the tip of his nightcap flapped in the cold wind. "I would know your face anywhere, sir; I have your portrait in my study. This is a very great honor!"

Copernicus shook Galileo's hand, looking more puzzled than pleased, and then he stared at Layla and Jess.

"Am I dreaming?" he asked.

"We're very glad to meet you, Copernicus," said Layla. "Will you come with us in our van? We're meeting lots of people you're going to like, and you might learn something!"

"I would be delighted to show you my telescope," said Galileo, still shaking Copernicus's long, bony hand. "I'm a very great admirer of yours, you see, and I'm trying to tell the world about heliocentrism."

"And is the world listening?" asked Copernicus, raising an eyebrow.

"Not yet," Galileo admitted, looking slightly disappointed, "but I'm hopeful," he added.

"I think they like each other," said Layla to Jess as Copernicus admired Galileo's telescope. "So which astronomer shall we fetch next?"

"What about Pythagoras?" said Jess, racking her brain. "He's the one who thought Earth was surrounded by crystal spheres. If anyone needs an astronomy lesson, it's him!"

Copernicus and Galileo suddenly stopped discussing heliocentrism.

"Pythagoras's model was wrong," Copernicus said, glaring sternly at Jess.

"It was utter balderdash," Galileo agreed, frowning at Layla.

"We don't like him," said Copernicus.

"We don't want him," said Galileo, "and he's not coming on our journey."

"You sound like squabbling schoolboys," said Jess. "We're going to see him whether you like it or not, because we need him for our homework. We need Aristotle too, and Thales and Anaximander."

"And Aristarchus," Layla added.

"Oooh, I'd like to meet Aristarchus," Copernicus said. "He almost had it right."

"I'd like to meet Aristarchus too," agreed Galileo.

Copernicus and Galileo seemed to agree about everything. It was getting a little boring, but Jess and Layla had a feeling that fetching the other astronomers would change all that.

"Copernicus," Layla said in a serious voice, "are you wearing your seat belt?"

"If you mean the flexible manacle, then yes, Galileo helped me with it," said Copernicus.

"Then let's go!" said Layla.

You Are Wrong!

Despite being parked in a peaceful corner of ancient Greece, under the shade of a tall cypress tree, Jess and Layla couldn't hear themselves think. There were seven astronomers in the back of the van now, and they were all yelling at each other.

"Of course Earth isn't round!" shouted Thales.

"I never said it was round, you silly old goat," Anaximander shouted back, "I said it was *cylindrical!*"

"Young man, I am your teacher and I know best."

"La, la, la!" Anaximander was pressing his hands firmly to his ears and singing, "I'm not listening, I'm not listening."

Meanwhile, Aristotle was glaring at Copernicus, shaking his head. "*Earth* is the center of the universe, sir—how dare you suggest that I am wrong!"

"I suggest that you are wrong because you are *clearly* wrong," said Copernicus loudly before adding, "or is your brain in your beard?"

"If it is," said Aristotle, sneering at Copernicus's smooth chin, "then that means you must have no brain at all!"

"In addition," said Copernicus pompously, ignoring Aristotle to his annoyance, "I think you'll find that the planets *do* orbit in a perfect circle."

"I agree with Copernicus," said Galileo, stabbing a finger in the air.

"Well, surprise, surprise," said Aristotle in a sarcastic voice.

"He's the only one talking sense around here," said Aristarchus, suddenly chiming in and pointing at Copernicus. "Him and that one with the long brown stick," he added as he stroked his long white beard.

"My name is Galileo," said Galileo, stepping forward, "and I think you'll find it's not a stick, it's a telescope."

41

Pythagoras, at this moment, was the only astronomer not arguing with anyone since he was far too busy staring through the window at the back of the van. "Listen to the music of the spheres," he said in a dreamy voice, "such lovely music."

"This is giving me a headache, Layla," Jess eventually announced. "I think we should take them all back home. Seriously, no homework is worth this much trouble."

Layla was fiddling around with the van's controls, trying to ignore the bickering astronomers, and as she fiddled she realized there was a button on the

dashboard that she had never seen before that said FULL BLAST.

"What do you think this button does, Jess?" Layla asked.

"By the look of things, it turns on the air-conditioning," Jess said, peering at it.

"It turned on the air-conditioning *before* the van became a time machine," said Layla, "or at least it did when the air-conditioning worked, years ago, but what does it do *now?*"

"I don't know, but something tells me you're going to press it anyway," sighed Jess.

Layla flashed Jess a smile and then jammed her thumb down hard on the button. There was a powerful flash of pure white light, and suddenly the astronomers stopped arguing and grabbed their seat belts as the van rocketed upward.

"Oooh!" gasped six of the seven astronomers.

"Lovely music," said Pythagoras, still staring dreamily out the window.

The van zoomed straight up into the air, tossing violently from side to side.

"Help!" shouted the astronomers, rattling around in the back of the van like coins in a jar.

The higher they traveled, the darker the sky grew. Then suddenly the heating in the van came on with a buzzing sound that made Aristarchus jump and look under his seat, confused.

"Where are we going?" Jess asked, clinging to her seat.

"It looks as though we're going into space," gasped Layla.

"But space travel in a van is IMPOSSIBLE!" shouted Jess.

"You thought time travel was impossible when you woke up this morning," laughed Layla, "but here we are!"

The van burst through the atmosphere and into the darkness beyond as the blue and green surface of Earth curved below them.

"Ha, I *told* you that Earth wasn't flat, Thales," crowed Anaximander, pressing his nose to the window while Thales stared out the window moodily, trying to hide that he was upset.

The farther the van flew, the rounder Earth appeared, until soon it was a beautiful blue and green ball, glowing in the darkness.

"It's a sphere!" Aristotle shouted, waving his arms in the air. "It's not a cylinder, Anaximander—it's a *sphere*, just as I thought!"

Anaximander, distraught, burst into tears so Jess handed him a tissue. Meanwhile, the van rocketed onward toward the Moon.

"I don't believe it!" Copernicus said. "The Moon has a rough surface!"

"My goodness, I always thought it was smooth," said Aristarchus as he peered over Copernicus's shoulder, "like a gemstone."

"So did I," Aristotle said, and they all nodded in agreement.

"Finally they agree about something," said Layla to Jess as they joined the astronomers at the window.

"Come and look, Galileo," said Copernicus. "The Moon appears to be very rough!"

"Oh, I don't need to," Galileo boasted. "You see, my telescope told me that the Moon was rough *years* ago."

As they passed Mars, Layla turned the steering wheel toward the vast reddish planet up ahead. "Let's take a little detour," she said.

"Goodness me, can that be Jupiter?" asked Aristarchus.

"In 1610, my telescope identified four moons orbiting Jupiter," boasted Galileo, suddenly having a run of being right.

"That's impossible," said Aristotle with scorn, "because *everything* orbits *Earth*."

"Look at the Great Red Spot on Jupiter," said Jess, trying to avoid yet another argument breaking out. "It's a huge storm that's been raging for hundreds of years."

"Oooh," said the astronomers, in unison.

They stared at the swirling storm on Jupiter's surface as the van hurtled past it, toward the farthest planets of the solar system. Everyone gasped at the beautiful rings around Saturn and Uranus, and the Sun grew smaller and smaller in the vast blackness of the universe.

"And that's the end of our solar system," Layla announced to the astronomers when the cloudy blue surface of Neptune came into view. "We hope you enjoyed your trip through space."

"Aw," said the astronomers in disappointment.

"Well, it's not quite the end," said Jess. "There did used to be a planet called Pluto beyond Neptune, but in 2006 it was reclassified as a dwarf planet instead."

"Poor Pluto," said Aristotle. "Imagine not being a proper planet!"

"I imagine it's a bit like not being a proper astronomer," Galileo muttered, not quite under his breath, looking at Aristotle.

Aristotle folded his arms and glared at Galileo. "For the last time, everything orbits EARTH," he said.

"I'm sorry to disappoint you, Aristotle," Layla said, "but you *are* wrong, and I think I can prove it. Now, I hope everybody is ready, because you're going to love this!"

And with that, Layla reached down with one foot and pressed the gas pedal, shooting the van way beyond the solar system.

Proof at Last

The van hovered above the solar system while the astronomers pressed their noses to the windows to watch the planets turning. In the middle, the Sun stayed perfectly still, like the eye of a storm or the center of a wheel.

"What is this madness?" Aristotle scoffed.

"These planets are making an oval shape as they orbit the Sun, not a perfect circle," gasped Copernicus, as he stared out the window for a closer look with his bony hands pressed to the glass. "Pythagoras, you even got *that* wrong."

"A friend of mine, Johannes Kepler, told me about oval orbits, but I didn't believe him," said Galileo sadly.

"You think you have problems?" Aristotle asked. "My whole theory is apparently incorrect!" And with that he burst into tears.

"Relax and listen to the music!" said Pythagoras.

"There *is* no music in the universe, you fool," snapped Copernicus.

Jess decided that she didn't like Copernicus very much, so she interrupted. "Well, actually, I think you'll find there *is* music in the universe. In 2014, a probe landed on a comet orbiting the Sun between Earth and Mars, and the probe picked up a noise the comet was making, which some people described as singing."

Pythagoras beamed with delight. "Music!" he said. "I wasn't wrong about everything!"

Aristotle sniffled. "I want to go home," he moaned.

"So do I," said Aristarchus.

"I have a *lot* of work to do," said Thales, stroking his beard thoughtfully.

"Me too," Anaximander sighed. "I'll have to rewrite everything!"

Galileo was polishing the lens of his telescope with the tip of his nightcap. Apart from Pythagoras, who was humming happily, the rest of the astronomers looked a bit sad, and Layla started to feel guilty.

"Maybe we shouldn't have taken the astronomers into space and shown them their mistakes," she said to Jess. "What will happen if they change their theories when they get back home?"

"Then I guess the history of astronomy will change forever," Jess answered.

Layla felt uncomfortable as the van turned toward home. She didn't want to change history, she thought, as the van rocketed away from Neptune.

"Good-bye, pretty rings," said Anaximander as they passed Uranus and Saturn.

"Good-bye, Great Red Spot," said Thales as they passed Jupiter's Great Red Spot.

Approaching Earth again, Layla made sure that the clock was set to Thales and Anaximander's time, and brought the van down through the atmosphere until they were safely parked beside the glittering Adriatic Sea in Greece. Seagulls squawked overhead while crabs investigated the van's rubber tires.

"Hey, let's give everyone a present," Jess suggested, "like a souvenir—that's bound to cheer them up!"

Layla and Jess hunted through their pockets, checked the glove box, and opened the overhead lockers in the back of the van, looking for presents to give their passengers.

They gave Thales a picnic plate, a nod to his theory that the world was flat. Anaximander received a can of beans from the van's tiny store cupboard for obvious reasons, though he didn't seem to know what to do with it. Layla passed Galileo the polishing cloth from her father's spare glasses that he kept on the dashboard, thinking it would be useful for his telescope, while Aristarchus accepted a pencil. Pythagoras received a bell from Waffles's old dog collar, and

Copernicus was given a small bag of pretzels from the glove box. Layla felt so bad about Aristotle that she gave him her watch, which he accepted, still sniffling.

"Good-bye, Thales and Anaximander," Layla said nervously as Jess opened the van door. "Forget all about us and write your theories so that future astronomers can study them—could you do that, please?"

As the earliest astronomers stepped down from the van onto the soft sand, a strange look passed across Thales and Anaximander's faces.

Thales gazed at the plate in his hands and said to Anaximander, "I have an idea. This plate—Earth—I have to go!"

Anaximander stared at his can of beans and said, "I also have an idea! This object, I think—Earth—I have to go too!"

The two astronomers hurried off in opposite directions, not glancing back at the van once.

"They've already forgotten about us," said Jess in delight. "This is great, Layla—it means we didn't change history at all!"

The same thing happened with Pythagoras and Aristotle. Aristarchus walked away, thoughtfully twirling his pencil between his fingers and muttering something about writing a book, while Copernicus munched on his pretzels as he walked back inside his house. Galileo got straight into bed with his telescope and pulled the blankets over the tip of his nightcap.

"Now all we have to do is write about it," said Layla as she twisted the clock dial back to 2015. The van zoomed up and away, back through time and space until it landed safely outside Layla's house.

"Dr. Goggles will never believe us," said Jess as they ran inside.

"We don't need her to believe us," Layla pointed out, "as long as she gives us a good grade so we're not at the bottom of the class!"

As they filed into class on Monday morning, Jess and Layla saw that Dr. Goggles had pinned pictures of all the astronomers they had been talking about around the walls of the science laboratory. Layla grinned at the marble sculptures of Thales and Anaximander, and she wondered whether Pythagoras was still humming and whether Galileo's extra-clean telescope meant that he was making even bigger discoveries.

Seeing all the pictures reminded Layla of their fantastic adventure, and the best part was that she and Jess hadn't changed history one bit.

"Leave your homework assignments on my desk, please," said Dr. Goggles.

"That was a really dumb assignment," Danny Philips complained. "Who wants to know about a bunch of old guys who were all wrong anyway?"

"Copernicus ate my homework," said Jade Jefferson, giving a feeble excuse for why she hadn't bothered to do the assignment.

Layla and Jess handed in their joint assignment and sat down. A picture of Aristotle gazed down at Layla from the wall beside her desk, and she giggled at his stern expression. Then she froze.

"What's the matter, Layla?" asked Jess.

"Aristotle!" gasped Layla. "You won't believe it, Jess, but . . . *he's wearing my watch!*"

Astronomers' Time Line

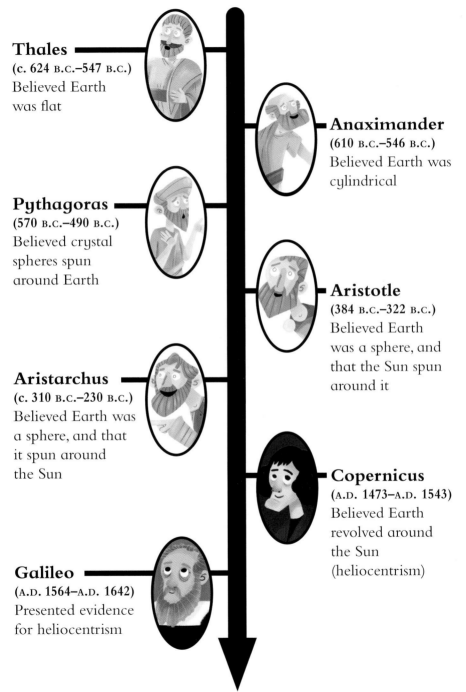

Thales
(c. 624 B.C.–547 B.C.)
Believed Earth
was flat

Anaximander
(610 B.C.–546 B.C.)
Believed Earth was
cylindrical

Pythagoras
(570 B.C.–490 B.C.)
Believed crystal
spheres spun
around Earth

Aristotle
(384 B.C.–322 B.C.)
Believed Earth
was a sphere, and
that the Sun spun
around it

Aristarchus
(c. 310 B.C.–230 B.C.)
Believed Earth was
a sphere, and that
it spun around
the Sun

Copernicus
(A.D. 1473–A.D. 1543)
Believed Earth
revolved around
the Sun
(heliocentrism)

Galileo
(A.D. 1564–A.D. 1642)
Presented evidence
for heliocentrism